For my dad,
who still doesn't like squirrels.

ISBN: 979-8-4438-3020-9

Welcome to the world of *Math Is Nuts*.
PEMDAS and SADMEP are two squirrels
learning to navigate tricky mathematical concepts.

Look for more titles in the *Math Is Nuts* series on
Amazon
and find more resources at
MathIsNuts.com.

Thank you for reading!

PEMDAS   **SADMEP**

"Spring is coming!" SADMEP said,
one cool but sunny day.
"The daffodils are sprouting.
Let's get our garden underway."

"A garden?" PEMDAS asked,
not sure there was a need.
"But we get all our veggies from Farmer Kevin,
as long as he doesn't see."

"Now, now," said the other squirrel.
"That isn't exactly fair.
We can grow our favorites,
plus have more to share!"

So PEMDAS and SADMEP planted their crops:
Dug the dirt and sowed the seeds.

Before they knew it, they had to harvest
much more than any squirrel needs.

"Let's share with our friends," said SADMEP,
"we can start by repaying the farmer."

"Even better," PEMDAS said,
"we'll share our gifts in groups of seven
in Farmer Kevin's
honor."

Seven stalks of rhubarb for one farmer.

"Now three groups of seven," SADMEP said.
"This rainbow chard looks nice."

"Twenty-one leaves.
That's just right
for our neighbor family of mice."

Seven stalks of rhubarb for one farmer.

"That was fun," young PEMDAS beamed.
"Who will we share with now?"

"My aunt and uncle eat a lot of salad,
more than anyone you've ever seen."

"Two groups of seven lettuce leaves —
that's a total of fourteen!"

Two squirrels, and each one gets seven lettuce leaves.
Two groups of seven makes fourteen in all.

"Now three groups of seven," SADMEP said.
"This rainbow chard looks nice."

"Twenty-one leaves.
That's just right
for our neighbor family of mice."

Three mice, seven leaves of chard each.
Three groups of seven, if you count them up,
make twenty-one.

"This is great," PEMDAS said,
"but it takes a while, I must say.
If I count the groups and the total we need,
we'll be here all day."

9...10...
11...

"Indeed," SADMEP told her friend,
"there is an easier way."

"I know what to do," replied PEMDAS,
his mouth curving into a smile.
"I'll simply add seven to the last number we had!"

"Let's try that for a while."

7

$7 + 7 = 14$

$14 + 7 = 21$

$21 + 7 = ?$

$7, 14, 21, ?$

Adding seven to the last number makes a pattern.
Can you tell what number is coming next?

"We can share our asparagus now.
We don't want to pick it too late."

"The rabbits will love it,
but they've hopped to work.
Just leave it at the gate."

Four rabbits, and each one eats
seven stalks of asparagus.
By PEMDAS' strategy, 21 + 7 = 28

"Now 28 plus seven, makes 35 of…these…"

"They're fancy radicchio, dear PEMDAS,
so be careful with them, please."

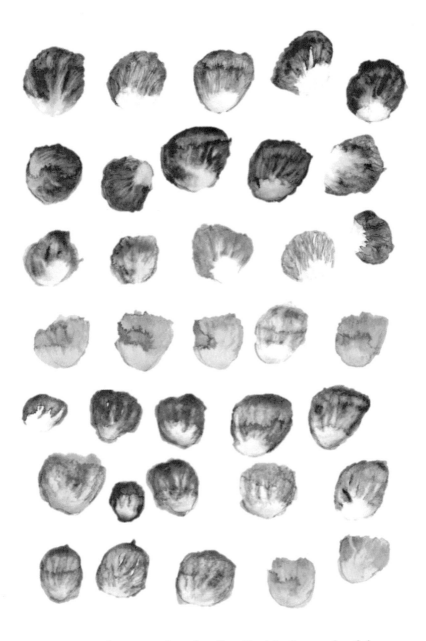

Five squirrels, seven heads of radicchio for each of them.
By PEMDAS' strategy, 28 + 7 = 35

"You're doing a great job," SADMEP said,
"but I can see you're tired by your eyes.

"I think it's time I told you:
For the big numbers, it's best to memorize."

"Really?" PEMDAS gasped,
"I thought I should always count."

"You can when you're learning," SADMEP said gently,
"and when you need to double check.
But I'm sharing the strategy that's best for me,
and some day it might save your neck."

1	2	3	4		6	7	8	9	10	11	12
1	1	2	3	4	5	6	7	8	9	10	11	12
2	2	4	6	8	10	12	14	16	18	20	22	24
3	3	6	9	12	15	18	21	24	27	30	33	36
4	4	8	12	16	20	24	28	32	36	40	44	48
5	5	10	15	20	25	30	35	40	45	50	55	60
6	6	12	18	24	30	36	42	48	54	60	66	72
7	7	14	21	28	35	42	49	56	63	70	77	84
8	8	16	24	32	40	48	56	64	72	80	88	96
9	9	18	27	36	45	54	63	72	81	90	99	108
10	10	20	30	40	50	60	70	80	90	100	110	120
11	11	22	33	44	55	66	77	88	99	110	121	132
12	12	24	36	48	60	72	84	96	108	120	132	144

Trace your finger along the top row to the number 7. Place your other finger on the number you want to multiply by in the first column. Bring your top finger down and left finger across until they meet, and you've found your answer!

$$7 \cdot 5 = 35$$

"Green beans for you and you and you —
seven times six is forty-two."

"How did you do that?" PEMDAS said,
"that was so fast, like the blink of an eye."

"That's how it goes, my friend,
when you learn to multiply."

$7 \cdot 6 = 42$

"Rabbits think carrots are just divine.
Seven times seven makes forty-nine."

"Seven times eight is fifty-six.
Cucumbers look like fat green sticks."

"Seven times nine is sixty-three.
Radishes are roots,
they don't come from trees."

"Ten rabbits,
each with seven broccoli.
That makes a total of seventy."

"And seven times eleven is seventy-seven.
With that many raspberries,
we'll be in heaven."

"Seven times twelve is eighty-four.
Counting all those peas would be a chore."

"We did it," said PEMDAS, with startling glee.
"Thank you, SADMEP,
for all your help and teaching me."

"We did it together," his friend replied,
"and we made lots of friends and
neighbors happy, too.
Now get some rest, then practice multiplying
till it's easy for you!"

	1	2	3	4	5	6	7	8	9	10	11	12
1							7					
2							14					
3							21					
4							28					
5							35					
6							42					
7	7	14	21	28	35	42		56	63	70	77	84
8							56					
9							63					
10							70					
11							77					
12							84					

Ideas for fun practice:

1. Go back through the paintings of fruits and vegetables and use a pencil to circle groups of seven.
Count how many groups there are on each page.
2. Erase and circle different groups. For example, groups of six green beans. How many groups are there?
3. Make up your own rhyme for each of the multiplication facts.
Try saying them while clapping, jumping rope, or brushing your teeth.
4. Do you have a garden or know someone who does?
Offer to help share the harvest in groups of seven.
5. Copy this times table and fill it in.
Make another with your favorite colors.

	1	2	3	4	5	6	7	8	9	10	11	12
1							7					
2							14					
3							21					
4							28					
5							35					
6							42					
7	7	14	21	28	35	42	49	56	63	70	77	84
8							56					
9							63					
10							70					
11							77					
12							84					

Find more resources at MathIsNuts.com.